SOUL BLOSSOMS

Soul Blossoms

Solee MacIsaac

EVERY BOOK PRESS

MMXXV

Book Design:
William Bentley

INTRODUCTION

Soul Blossoms is a collection of observations through the lens of a nubile soul attempting to understand this life. All directions herein are to myself, or to those that can use them. In the contract with the reader disagreements are allowed; the intention is to create a space to absorb contradictions. If anything penetrates, please know it comes with love.

Solee MacIsaac

Soul Blossoms *is dedicated to my daughter, Joanna Parks, whose struggling soul, at times, shows bursts of brilliant light.*

Once again, a big Thank You to my husband, a fine poet, who puts aside his own work to address mine. Editor in Chief – I am grateful.

Growth in higher spheres,
Though invisible,
Germinates in fertile soul.

SOUL BLOSSOMS

The wide horizon
Opens before me,
I am here.

Begin again,
Life persists;
A journey home, interrupted.

Hungry for spirit life,
Filled with light,
Attending to daily necessities.

Meeting together,
Sharing our light,
Open to higher plane.

Childlike innocence,
Wondering and wandering,
With wide open eyes.

Old body,
Older soul,
   Lady in waiting.

Sweet baby soul
Needing schooling,
   Too many wants.

Tender moments
Fly,
   Before the face of reality.

Bonded to eternity,
Temporarily stuck
In temporal existence.

Like fly paper
I'm stuck to it,
It sticks to me.

Joy in breathing,
Relishing light,
Sweet to feel heartbeat.

Grateful for life,
Grateful for respite from life,
Ever grateful.

Raw fish,
Green tea,
Life isn't so bad.

Events happen
All the time;
Experiencing them, sometimes.

The apple
So smooth:
    Red, round and firm.

No wonder
Eve was tempted...
    Fragrant, colorful food.

Contemplating existence,
Digging deeper,
    Quick, tomato is rolling away.

Navel inquiries,
Center around
Your center.

Don't drag it out,
Say what you mean,
There really is so little time.

Everything is a test,
Every moment
A new doorway opens.

White hot days
Recede into
A trembling Autumn.

Melting greens
Traded for reds and golds,
Trees waving like flags.

Fires boldly causing havoc,
Turmoil in households,
Keep calm and proceed.

Thoughts, feelings,
Strange associations,
Where and when am I bound?

Staying on the right track,
More complex
Than originally expected.

Not enough gratitude
To cover
The help received.

Thoughts whizz by,
Electronic and dangerous;
    Sink into cool quiet presence.

Even the crickets
Know when to stop
    Chirping.

Moving in and out of
Light and shadow,
    Some things seen, some not.

Consistency is key
To staying in the light;
Keyhole is right before you.

We want a hand up,
Which we receive,
And often don't realize it.

Some people, seen through
Eyes of love,
Are just perfect.

"Never enough," say the queens.
"More than enough," say the kings.
"Enough is enough," says the steward.

Unadorned beauty,
Essence in youth,
Like the sweetest rosebud.

Dry cracked days,
Heat oppression,
Another season looming.

Revelry, song and dance,
Red roses,
Flying across the stage.

When all is done,
You are
What is left.

End of Summer,
Tired trees,
Drooping leaves and thistles.

In the east,
Trees are about to bloom,
Like a rainbow bouquet.

Time to withdraw,
Assess all acquired,
Digest and integrate.

Build a sanctum
In the invisible world
Via moments of intense reality.

When the sea stops moving,
And the sun sets in the East,
    I will no longer love Nature.

Cats on the roof,
Again,
    View must be amazing.

Rain, hard to believe,
Rain, soft, cool, wet,
    In August, so strange.

Without this body,
Its talents, its flaws…
Who shall I be?

How came I?
From where?
Where will I go?

The inside me,
Sees beauty, courage,
Pain and suffering.

The outside me,
Smiles and says, "It's fine."
What is really real?

In the harsher moments of life,
Deeper thoughts emerge,
Silk curtains melt away.

Only one thing is certain,
One thing on which to stand,
Everything else is false.

Morning again,
Rotations of Earth
Make me dizzy.

Some mornings
It is difficult
To stay positive.

Greet each moment
With the best You,
Stay real.

Chip away at judgement,
Trust love,
Use patience against irritation.

Sweet moment of release,
From all issues,
Divine light arrests discord.

We know enough
To realize
Help is absolutely necessary.

The peaceful inner space
That contains my present self,
    Quiets the clamoring below.

To continually live
In that space,
    Is devoutly to be wished.

As the ancients
Have already said it all,
    Fabulous to understand them.

The pathway
Is firmly tread,
But few have taken it.

Patience, persistence,
Moderation, and consistency,
Are preferred virtues.

Imitated emotions
Are worthless,
Save energy for real ones.

Momentary life
May seem small,
But is, what is remembered.

A baby, a beginning,
Or not?
A beginning for parents, maybe.

Beginnings and endings,
Have nothing in common
With circles.

Here to do work, find wisdom,
Garner moments of presence,
Serve as best as possible.

Above all,
Love presence,
And be grateful.

Life is a trick,
Things that appear important,
Are usually nothing at all.

What inside us falls for it?
Weakness? Imitation?
Inability to perceive truth?

Seems necessary to be kind,
Carry on with inner work,
Appreciate opportunity to live.

Others go through difficulties,
Help and support them
With compassion and love.

None of us are alone,
Though loneliness is felt,
    Another illusion.

We see the blossom,
But know nothing of what
    The bud went through.

Seeing through the glamour
Of a glossy world,
    Helps prevent confusion.

There is good to be found,
If there is Good
Looking for it.

The visible world
Tantalizing and disappointing,
Has lessons and opportunities.

The invisible world
Has depth and meaning,
From which all things appear.

Myths and legends
Point to the invisible world;
  Easily construed as fantasy.

Friends come together gladly,
And enjoy sharing;
  Part with new understandings.

So much is learned
By surrendering
  Vanity and willfulness.

The day's end
Is simple and complete;
      Space is left for tomorrow.

The quiet and unobtrusive
Can be overlooked,
      But actually sees everything.

If I could change anything
In the past,
      I would have been quieter.

Why are we afraid?
If even death
Is a blessing?

It's easy to fall in a hole,
Just step
In the wrong place.

Enlightened minds,
Only useful coupled with
Enlightened hearts.

Reminders are helpful,
But actually it is necessary
    To mind the reminders.

It all depends on the light
You can absorb
    And radiate.

Following a teacher's path,
Doesn't help without
    Following his instructions.

It is so lucky
To understand the need
For conscious light.

Great, indeed,
Is the holy present space,
Between the brows.

Our real inner lives
Are invisible to many,
But are revealed to each other.

Empathy and compassion
Are important tools;
   Real sharing outclasses them.

Love, not easy to find,
Like the fish, "What water?"
   Love supports air we breathe.

Be pure like the water of life,
Let no obstacles impede
   The flow of love and presence.

In a way,
Serving is following
The path of least resistance.

In the end,
Things as they are,
Myself as I am.

Many factors helped frame
Our essence;
Baseline for inner work.

Higher centers have a life
Unrelated to the hectic
Lower centers.

Salty tears
That fill up the sea,
Cannot move a frozen heart.

A budding soul
Struggles for the light,
As do all young things.

Time: an opportunity,
Or a trial,
    Depending upon patience.

Forgiveness is for ourselves,
Others do fine without it,
    We judge and must forgive.

Around the world,
Our special lights,
    Enhance the globe.

We grace each other,
And ourselves,
With our presence.

Old ways,
Need to be discarded,
In favor of the present moment.

Each moment
Is new,
Even if we are not.

The overarching light
Is being conscious
Itself.

Slipping into old self happens,
As it is habitual;
Be fresh as each moment.

Rilke loved the questions,
We must be
The answers.

Preparation helps,
Ready for divine intervention:
A stupendous achievement.

What makes pleasant evening,
The setting, the meal?
Yes, but really, it's the company.

Ordinary is only
What we become inured to,
Things are truly extraordinary.

Seeing point of light,
In darkest night,
Is beginning of understanding.

No one else can tell you
Who you really are,
Self-awareness is from Self.

Loving one's Self,
Is the source and destination
Of conscious Love.

Birthdays and anniversaries,
Celebrating acknowledgment
Of time and dear connections.

Bruised and stained,
Forging ahead,
Baby soul sprouting wing buds.

Circulation of energy
Within a school of accolades,
Is swift and highly beneficial.

Watching stars
Piercing night sky,
Movement seems imperceptible.

Changing perspective
Can reveal subjectivity,
With acceptance.

Life has ups and downs,
If we allow them;
Being consistent is a treasure.

Mood swings are indulgence
No longer afforded,
Expensive for limited energy.

So much precious energy
Is squandered in youth,
Age teaches frugality.

We are both old and young
At the same time,
Moving in two directions.

In this timeless moment,
Nothing else
    Seems to matter.

Learning never stops,
Transformation of experiences
    Produces wisdom.

Preparing for an event,
Presence now,
    So there can be presence later.

Imagining some moments
Are more important,
　　Sans presence they are same.

Everything feels speeded up;
Must slow down inside,
　　To catch up.

Stumbling but not quite falling,
Reaching for help to stay even:
　　Want less, appreciate more.

Feeling prickly,
Calming agitated emotions,
Can be like herding cats.

How typical, becoming upset
Over something meaningless,
Only presence is meaningful.

A vagabond on the Earth,
We visit such a short time,
And think that we own things.

The Earth knows nothing
Of boundaries,
　　Humans compartmentalize life.

Our worlds sometimes collide,
When truth intrudes,
　　And reveals reality.

Caring for each other
Extends into invisible world,
　　Love more than hearts can hold.

Without a school and school work,
People get by, somehow;
So much is left to chance.

Thank everything, everyone
That allowed you to be
Where you are right now.

Everything depends upon
Realizing absolute necessity
To be present to one's life.

A river of love
Washes through our school,
    And travels around the globe.

Share a meal with a friend,
Share a moment together,
    Present moments are perfect.

The gift of conscious light
Cannot be conceived
    Without infinite gratitude.

The crickets are extra loud,
They know Summer
　　Is nearing its end.

September begins with rain,
Plants are happy,
　　A welcome reprieve from heat.

We might wish to remove pain
From a fellow traveler,
　　But know nothing of their play.

Love and emotional support
Is welcome;
Each person has their lesson.

We will journey into Fall,
Traveling east together,
Flying to parts unknown.

Emotional limits get stretched
In order to sustain
Tremendous charge of love.

The desert of imagination
Holds dangerous critters,
Best to stay in the light.

Like smoking or over-drinking,
Imagination is a bad habit,
And bad choice over Presence.

Wishing to escape reality,
Beings have never really
Experienced it.

Do we affect the weather,
The way it affects us?
We are just as changeable.

Books and people
Hold many experiences;
Books are consistent in report.

School is larger than teacher,
And students,
The faculty is mostly invisible.

Writing is slow work;
Muse is not always available.
　　Patience is part of endeavors.

True Presence does not need
Anything else,
　　It is its own reward.

Living the truth
In an ideal state of being,
　　Simplifies actions, experiences.

Children holding hands,
Dancing into sunrise,
Teaches volumes about reality.

We are more joined than ever,
What is separate and different,
Is less and less meaningful.

The ever-refreshing light
Of conscious reality,
Floods our being when awake.

Thoughts aren't bad,
But can be distractions,
From quiet presence.

When the psyche
Finally realizes its true home,
Complications seem farcical.

Many connections are brief,
Yet all contribute to the whole
Electric body of the school.

Grateful for each other,
We are here
Because we are present.

If you feel that things
Are happening through you,
Not by you, you are right.

A rich silence awaits
The exhausted soul,
Upon giving up pretense.

Worrying about other people's
Opinions of us or others,
    Is a fruitless, wasteful expense.

Attempt to correct mistakes,
Useful, but not
    At the expense of presence.

Arguments are like two
Desert windstorms,
    Colliding.

Usually nothing real
Is accomplished,
Except energy loss.

The inner sanctum
Of silent peace,
A refuge for lighted presence.

Presence aware of itself,
Is born of itself,
In the undying light.

Seeking happiness – normal,
But easily disappointing,
    Unless it is gleeful presence.

Work is not drudgery;
Work is the action
    Of a loving and grateful heart.

We stand atop
So many shoulders,
    Our luck is boundless.

The forgers of the path,
Cannot be thanked enough,
    We honor travelers before us.

Ultimate destination is close,
Drop all baggage,
    Enter true home.

School on Earth,
Is only kindergarten,
    Higher school, higher states.

New realms, new experiences,
Can engender fine energies;
Be present to catch everything.

We are given more than
We can usually absorb;
Shocks enlighten eyes.

Transformation
Is a way of
Life.

We are in this together,
Which helps,
Even if the plays are different.

It's not how long you are alive,
But how much of life,
You actually live.

Looking back,
How many moments
Are actually yours?

Much of our memory
Revolves around
    Shocks.

Higher forces are generous
In their attention
    To our sleep.

Eating, resting, working,
All provide opportunities,
    For realizing divine presence.

Walking into the sublime light,
Our real self emerges,
And we join eternal company.

Belief based on wishing.
Knowing based on experience.
Presence based on being.

There is no better
Present,
Than Presence.

Sometimes it is difficult
To see results from our efforts;
　　Results come unexpectedly.

Inaudible music from paradise
May haunt our dreams;
　　But it is no less real.

Angels have no voices,
They are harmonious eternally,
　　And communicate simply.

Music is direct for us,
It can bypass the intellect,
    And go straight to the heart.

In our silence,
Bright light fills the need
    For speech.

Arrows to the heart,
Transformed,
    Create a love bouquet.

Energy contained
And used for presence,
    Is a self-perpetuating source.

Controlled and intentional
Movements of the body,
    Can be a beautiful expression.

Unintentional movements
Are often
    Frenetic, weak, and unpleasant.

A painter
Who randomly uses his brush,
  Will not define his subject.

Even chickens have a life,
Before they become
  Someone's dinner.

Appreciating beauty, typical.
Appreciating service, graceful.
  Appreciating presence, rare.

Day's beginning and ending,
Seem to whizz by
In an increasing velocity.

So much of life seems artless,
It is our job to add
Intention, awareness, presence.

Conscious light
Brings reality into focus,
Oh, joyous sight!

Dry leaves are already
Drifting to my doorway,
   Fall weather approaching.

Soon comes introspection
And being especially grateful,
   For all that has gone before.

Summer events, fun, exciting,
Autumn is cool and tranquil,
   Winter is closeness, coziness.

Changes on different scales
Affect us continually;
    Best to keep inner stillness.

Friends come and go,
One thing remains,
    And is ever fresh and new.

Like love,
How could presence
    Ever be old.

Appreciation for art
May be subjective,
Objective art pierces the heart.

If you can't understand
Simply,
It is unnecessarily complex.

Be brief,
Be simple,
BE.

Like a baby learning
To walk and talk,
    A fledgling soul picks its way.

Each moment presents
A new opportunity,
    A new challenge.

Unexpected events,
Positive or negative,
    Can be used for presence.

When fatigued we recharge
With rest and food;
Higher fuels difficult to acquire.

Finer and finer energies
Are available to those
Light and fine themselves.

The pain of another's suffering
Must also be transformed,
Even while helping them.

Patience my heart,
Life is both long and short,
Take it moment by moment.

Young beings
Can tax tranquility,
Use the excess energy to Be.

If this level is a reflection
Of a higher level,
What will our work be there?

Always more light,
Until all that we are
Is God.

The light is faint at times,
It is always there,
Whenever I reach for it.

There are twists and turns
To work through,
Emotions run high.

All is resolved
In silent
    Presence.

A new infant is hungry to grow,
A new rose breaks through
    Rough ground to sunlight.

A new soul is hungry
For uncreated light,
    To nurture ultimate refinement.

The garden of souls
Is planted and cared for
With great intention.

Harvest is not for us
To determine,
A higher agency picks date.

The higher world can examine
The lower one,
But why would it?

We aspire to what
We know is above us,
    Even though we cannot see it.

The only really bad thing,
Is the illusion,
    Of the prison of sleep.

The lower self
Has no friends, has no love,
    Has no possibilities.

Listening to its complaints,
Fears and suspicions,
Is a way to fall into illusion.

Presence is both
The result and the source
Of spiritual efforts:

A light that never diminishes,
A beacon to higher states,
A remedy for weary hearts.

The best of me,
Is not me at all,
But a sublime spark of God.

Moderation
Until the
Leap.

Remember the highs
When you are low,
And lows when you are high.

Extreme measures
Usually require expensive
Expenditures.

Keeping an even keel,
Is no small
Aim.

Dionysus has his place,
Divine madness
Is ultimate sanity.

With the two-direction arrow
Attention is not doubled,
It is squared.

The overarching light
Is above, only until
We rise to become it.

Fine energies shared
Become a tsunami
Of love.

Subjectivity is a trial,
Depicting granular
Understandings.

God sees through our eyes
When we are free
Of imagination.

We have known each other
Before,
Shared work made fast friends.

Learning temperance
Is a sign of maturity,
No matter the years lived.

Treat each sunrise
With reverence;
Another day of Presence.

Join your hands to remind
Head and heart
To be joined.

Child of my body,
Fellow traveler;
    Grateful to know you.

Being responsible
Is the ability to respond,
    To demands of the moment.

Shouldering the world
Is for Atlas,
    Let the river of life flow.

The universe is vast,
Time defines our small world,
  Space too huge to comprehend.

Science and mathematics
Have a language to describe
  What is beyond human scope.

Having knowledge
Is not the same
  As knowing.

In some ways, it is very simple,
Drop all complications:
Be.

Earning valuation
And conviction
Is the hard part.

Reach for the light: Be,
Refresh: Be,
Remember: Be.

Up where the air
Is rarified,
    See the realm of angels.

When the light is on
Don't keep looking
    For the switch.

There is beauty, cleanliness,
Friendship, and refinement
    To enjoy and promote.

Not everyone sees
The same way
　　As one's own subjectivity.

By listening with heart,
You can get a peek
　　Into another's world view.

Animals share our world
But each one has its own
　　Circular world view.

These concentric circles
Interpenetrating
Reflect whirling solar system.

Our essence is not separate
From nature,
Our miracle is divine blessing.

Life gobbles energy;
The higher one rises,
The finer the energy.

We must be fine to rise,
And be able to use
Fine energy.

If it seems a monumental task,
It is.
One moment at a time.

Kindness to others
Helps to keep focus away
From one's own lower self.

Men prefer to climb mountains
Than to keep their attention
    On their steps, breaths, lives.

Cooking is a good alchemy;
Mix foods, heat just right,
    Transform coarse ingredients.

Every action takes attention.
A powerful tool,
    Don't let it run amok.

Discretion applies to much,
While the moment is always
    Perfect.

Connections run deep
Between those who have
    Transformed friction together.

The angels are more attentive
To us,
    Than we are to each other.

What is most visible in us
To higher beings,
Is our inner desire to rise.

Presence brings us closer
To beings who are assigned
To help us be at their level.

The array of things offered
At life's marketplace,
Seems desperate for survival.

Organization is necessary;
Room for spontaneity,
Also necessary.

Beauty is beyond necessary;
In a state of grace,
Beauty is everywhere.

Throw your arms around
Your own possibilities,
Move forward courageously.

Trying to lose weight,
It seems I am eating more;
Someone is ambushing me.

This time,
"More is less"
Does not apply.

Don't underestimate
Denying force,
Each step includes presence.

We are born into this world,
Try to make our way,
Then slip out of it.

The "why" of it escapes us;
Without presence, a show
Signifying nothing.

To be truly oneself
Must include humility
And reverence.

It is difficult to see light,
Unless it is surface reflected,
Except inner uncreated light.

Soul growing is hard work,
There is no handbook.
Luckily, plenty of guidance.

There is no comparison
With others,
All the lessons are unique.

We are only held back
By our own judgement,
And fears.

In presence,
We are aware of the neutrality
Of events.

If you want more
And finer energies,
Stop the leaks.

Beings of light
Are pointing the way,
Light-filled, we follow.

A bud is sweet,
How much more
The blossom.

The mature soul fragrance
Must be an ecstatic
Perfume.

Traveling to distant friends,
Spreading love,
We gather all the light we can.

Beaming love,
The teacher reaches us all,
Unrelenting conscious light.

Our karmic lives
Continue on their fated paths,
Watch each moment in parallel.

Another year has made
Its way in me,
Time to reflect on gains, losses.

I am lighter,
Less sorrow,
More presence.

Being here
In this moment,
Is deceptively simple.

So much goes into
The ability to be present,
Even more is left out.

The Self nestled in presence
Finds refuge
And often delight.

We, the light bearers,
Carry our torches high,
Acknowledging our source.

It is necessary to honor
Our forefathers,
    If but to forestall vanity.

The pillars of this work
Have provided strong support
    For all we are able to Be.

We cannot underestimate
Sleep-inducing programming,
    We need a lot of help.

We have invisible help,
Also, an invisible enemy,
Continuing to work against us.

The more we are present,
The less space
Allowed for lower energies.

Watching yellow butterflies
Rise into the high blue,
Longing for freedom to fly.

My cat is also watching,
A good reminder
Of the Laws on this planet.

Sometimes this life
Feels like a story I am telling,
Similar to dreams at night.

Shocks help to keep
My feet on the ground,
And my heart and mind alive.

If I were to pray,
It would be to be able
To have more gratitude.

There is so much beauty
In the Fall,
Seasons offer changing treats.

Simple human pleasures
Can be a positive reminder
To be present to them.

Aroma of morning coffee,
Feel of silk across your arm,
Light filtering through trees.

It is fortunate to appreciate
Our lives through moments
Of presence.

Great is the work,
Before and behind me,
Small is the step this moment.

Friendship in the school,
Is based on much more
Than mere affection.

Learning to see difficulties
Not as disasters, but as
Means to a higher level.

Electrical currents run through
The web of connections
That is our School.

Everyone is helped
By one student's
        Advancement.

Soup, beautiful soup,
Warming,
        On a cool Fall day.

Life is simple,
Upon realizing higher powers
        Handle the big stuff.

Pain adds scale to moments,
Cancelling some 'I's,
Unfortunately, adds new ones.

Many fears and worries
Dissolve,
In the clear light of presence.

Inside take a step back,
Let the 'I's slide by,
They have nothing to offer.

The neutral place of observing
Is ever solid ground,
For springing upward.

Our states are variable,
Presence cuts through the
Chaos.

To be consistent
Requires
Presence.

Celestial bodies
Are not all planet-sized,
Many are beautiful people.

Invisible benefactors
Gather where presence
Shines like a beacon.

This plane of existence
Can seem cruel and painful,
Also astonishingly beautiful.

All becomes material
To be used,
    For divine presence.

It helps to practice
On happy and difficult days,
    Realizing none of that is us.

Like the Yin and Yang symbol,
There is always a grain
    Of the other – in any event.

As an orchestra gathers
For the grandest symphony,
    Our composition sounds.

The conductor
Listens carefully,
    And moderates.

We wish heaven
To hear and respond,
    And it does.

We are both
The procurers and the product,
   Of the miraculous.

Cool and diffuse,
Starlight,
   Is closest to uncreated light.

Blowing out candles on a cake,
For a moment,
   Feels strangely satisfying.

Photographs capture
A moment,
But do they, really?

Our own true self
Is the pathway to follow,
Ultimately, we are the truth.

After you've taken care
Of everything,
You still cannot control results.

Some puzzles are not meant
To be solved,
  Sometimes best to just drop it.

Love extends in the direction
Of the loved one,
  Conscious love shines globally.

Cold rain and gloom
Foretelling Winter;
  Time to hibernate.

Generosity
Stimulates like,
    In simpatico souls.

It is more than lucky
That we are together
    Here at the same time.

Good wine
Good company
    I am grateful.

It may be a sliding scale
That determines value,
   But true value is priceless.

What or who makes us
Who we are?
   Who am I really?

Inside I know who I am,
But forces I don't understand,
   Twist me into one I don't know.

To be the same person
Always,
Is much larger than it seems.

In a world of men and women,
Vanity reigns supreme,
An empty show, dressed nicely.

Dressing well is not a problem,
It's imagining a reality –
A non-existent center focus.

Cooking dinner for friends,
Feels good,
And tastes good, too.

Traveling across the globe
Time zones are scrambled
Until readjusting.

Out of patterns is good,
Still, a lot of preparation,
Just to remain same person.

We are best served,
Who learn to serve
    Well.

The highest service
We can provide,
    Is to remain present.

Here, we are granted
An allotment of time,
    To serve the highest.

The law of householder
Occupies us a great deal;
It mustn't overcome high aims.

The lower self is grim
And looks to the worst
In ourselves and in others.

It is often hidden,
When it shows itself,
Take a long look, remember.

Museums contain
Years of beauty condensed
Into a profound visit.

Preservation is a worthy aim,
If a high standard of value
Is used to discriminate.

In many paintings,
Women's flesh predominates,
As softness is temporal.

Capturing emotional moment
Through an artist's eye,
   Beyond a camera's capacity.

No matter what your name is
Your very last one
   Will be: Light.

Covered in ashes,
Preserved for ages,
   Artistic treasures slept.

Many secrets
Are revealed
In quiet moments.

Stop, look around,
Relax all but your
Awareness.

Innocent and knowing,
A crown of light surrounds
A generous heart.

She holds a third eye
In her hand,
And looks directly at me.

A simple act
Humble,
Yet glorified.

There is too much to see,
So much captured beauty,
Delightful moments of clarity.

Formalized religion fostered
Art and architecture,
And death and destruction.

We are the watchers
Of the Play,
Not the designers.

Bells are ringing,
People are singing,
Birds are winging.

Spain is so lovely,
Town on the mountaintop,
   Ronda of the white bull.

The spiral of life and death,
Has no beginning or ending,
   But it does have a center.

Always beginning,
We are first at everything,
   Lastly our real selves.

Roaring around the house
Wind desperate to get in;
    Frustrated, drags lawn chairs.

Madrid, Botin, roast piglet,
Red wine, lovely buildings,
    Encarnacion.

Last day,
Tomorrow we fly home,
    To Michael's wonderful recital.

Tea, British Museum,
Elgin Marbles,
        Many, many impressions.

Words can't encompass
The wonder of another
        Culture.

An ancient religion,
Relics of worship, reverence,
        Long forgotten.

Stone pillars,
Carved intricately,
Supporting nothing.

Grand edifice,
Gateway for the gods,
No one enters.

You have your moments
And then
You don't.

Falling leaves,
Blowing, streaming,
    Wind howling its pain.

Interruptions
Don't exist,
    It is only life manifesting.

Red vines creeping along
The bricks,
    Tendrils brushing my sleeve.

Benevolent beings
Support us,
Even when we are unforgiving.

Light kissed red-orange roses,
Fireplace glowing,
Sweet apples, crisp and juicy.

A pure heart is not affected
By sudden fortune,
Or peer praise.

The end of Autumn
Is sweet sadness,
    Shoring up for Winter.

Wish for what you have,
It could not be
    Better.

Gratitude Day,
Thanksgiving,
    Feast of positive harvest.

My body of light
Casts no shadow,
 And is weightless.

Morning light
Is especially promising,
 For the day ahead.

Each day, hour, minute, second
Is yours,
 If you claim it.

Mosaics from the ancients,
Reveal the timeless beauty
  Of a past age.

Humans are the same
Throughout time,
  Same foibles and strengths.

Sleep and death
Comes for all,
  Who avoid truth.

November chill
Seeps under my front door,
Harbinger of hoary Winter.

Old friends and new
Become the pathway
To greater understandings.

A lapse in emotional control,
Shows how fragile
The grasp of the present moment.

When judging
Remember who is
Judging who.

Stumbling on the path
Is better,
Than stumbling off the path.

War, negative emotions,
On the scale of countries,
Shows the degree of danger.

Wings of love,
Enfold us,
Every moment.

Resisting love
Is a strange place
In which we find ourselves.

Being empty of wants,
Leaves an opening
For love and light to enter.

Wordless beholding,
Presence filled,
   I greet you, my love.

Dawn piercing night clouds,
Hilly land rumbling awake,
   Reluctant to start another day.

We know what to do,
We know how to do it,
   All that remains is Will.

Be simple like a child,
Don't complicate
Complications.

Insight in retrospect,
May be helpful;
Uncreated light resolves issues.

Higher centers,
Are powerful joined together;
Behold, the Self appears.

Reality doesn't compromise
With wishes or imagination,
    Actual existence stands alone.

The landscape of world six
Unfolds instantaneously,
    In a moment of reality.

Many things are perceived,
Digestion and acceptance
    Can take time.

Long nights of wakefulness,
Can punish
A troubled mind.

Love and light softens
Negatively charged
Particles.

Dress in colors that reflect
Your joy,
Be a rainbow inside and out.

The inner and outer world
Aren't all that different,
    Try to stay in higher centers.

Acting too quickly,
Like eating unripe fruit:
    Disruptive consequences ensue.

Poetry, music, sculpture, art,
Interconnect via higher mind,
    And provide new insights.

Realizing our complete
Dependence on higher forces
Is a good place to start.

To be a good learner, essential,
Drop old modes of learning,
Allow the purity of silent space.

Past holds kernels of insight,
Future tantalizes imagination,
Present has real possibilities.

Bend low,
Acknowledge gratefully
All you are given.

Crumbling leaves everywhere,
Temperature drop,
Autumn has snuck up again.

Cinnamon fragrant kitchen,
Warm fire, snuggly slippers,
All enhance gratitude.

There is nothing
Outside of the
　　Present moment.

Even Love
Only exists
　　Now.

If sometimes
You don't recognize yourself,
　　It is because it was not You.

A good relationship
Starts with the one
    You have with yourself.

The role of a god
Though exalted,
    Isn't an easy one.

Fields of frost,
Steam rises with morning sun,
    Boots crunch brown leaves.

Money is helpful
To acquire necessities,
    Money itself is only paper.

In truth,
We are uncreated light,
    We are the gift of God.

Don't fall into the cycle
Of unexamined life,
    Sleep of imagination is death.

The staying power of presence
Comes from love of being,
   And fear of sleep.

The only fight worthwhile,
Is an internal struggle
   With your own imagination.

When higher centers appear,
All struggles disappear;
   Reality reigns.

Love whom you will,
We are all deserving of love,
    Salve and adornment of life.

Underneath everything,
Time sparks stress;
    Leaving time, the only option.

It is easy to see why
Green is the favorite color
    Of desert dwellers.

Encouragement is the blessed
Aspect
   Of motherhood.

It's not so simple,
And yet,
   It is.

Wealth is measured
In many ways,
   Wealth of spirit surpasses all.

Depth of experiences
Outweighs
Length of life.

Alone and lonely
Are not the same,
We are never really alone.

A little circle of cat
Formed on my lap,
Purring her song.

Get presence where you can,
Remember,
All is temporary.

Rain loves the earth and sky
So much,
It falls from one to the other.

Rivers love the ocean
So much,
That they run to join it.

Sunflowers turn their faces
To the beloved;
Daily prayers.

Hearts joined
In harmony
Emanate joy.

Buds with soul,
Budding souls,
Soul buddies – all accepted.

Breathe the rarified air
Of light bodies,
    Spread wings to the horizon.

Life isn't easy
There is only one
    Simple thing.

Seasons change,
Life moves along,
    Only one changeless thing.

Music follows it,
Sculpture, paintings,
   All art seeks harmony.

Sing all day,
Dance all evening,
   Hear the music all night.

What is new and old,
Depends upon
   Our point of view.

Pont Neuf
Is the oldest bridge
In Paris.

Mother and child,
Care and joy,
Love without strings.

Like a butterfly on the wing
We fly to beauty,
With love to give.

Don't resent
Freely given help,
    We all need it.

The magical alchemy
Of soul creation,
    Tragically defaults to lower self.

Heavens dispense
Their light
    As they see fit.

In the garden of delights,
Keep remembrance
Of your true self.

May what is good
Bless you
With light.

Everything needs us
To be released,
From the material prison.

Each moment provides
A chance for love
    To unchain Light.

The world is hard and fast,
We are fluid light,
    Waiting to serve.

There is nothing too small,
Too insignificant,
    To trust to present light.

We are in a new challenge
With no space or time,
    Only everything else.

Don't be afraid
Of the baby chicks,
    The loud cheeping is music.

To be God
Is ultimate
    Service.

Mother's love
Is a good start,
    Become mother to all.

Feed higher needs,
With love for
    Lower levels.

Truth hurts
Only what is
    Untrue.

The bud blooms
When it is ready,
    Patience is required.

Release struggle,
Let go of efforts,
    Allow reality to appear.

It's neither here nor there;
Contradictions fall away,
    When leaping scales.

Peace appears
At the point
Of unity.

No path, no journey,
No hurry, no limits,
Release fear, release self.

Catching yourself,
Being not yourself,
Is a too common foible.

What tender places
Do we avoid,
    By hiding in plain sight.

Stresses, strains,
Loyalty ties break!
    Trust only one thing.

Pick up the pieces,
Remember, it is not you,
    Who does any of it.

No blame, no applause.
Only courtesy, gratitude,
And genuine acceptance.

Feeling put upon
Is just wrong valuation,
Angels have pressure mandate.

The stronger we seem,
Others will lean against us,
Until we can no longer move.

The balance of forces
Not so easily perceived,
    Until they are out of balance.

Love, however,
Can always be given,
    And felt.

Cows don't know
They are someone's dinner,
    Just like us.

Fall leaves are so beautiful,
It is strange trees shed them,
Undressed in frigid Winter.

Come closer to the hearth,
Warm your hands,
Tell me the story of you.

We are growing old together,
Just as we planned,
Pain and joys shared alike.

We are so lucky,
Great compassion seeks us;
    Or we would be forever lost.

Everything is happening
Just one seat over,
    Move.

The pull of the world,
Though strong,
    Not as mighty as Death.

Be grasped by uncreated light,
It won't let go
As long as you do.

The body,
Cool and delicious,
The soul, so much more so.

Stop climbing the ladder;
Let go,
And fly.

Morning refreshes
With new possibilities,
    Except, unfinished yesterday.

Wishing can be exquisite pain,
Offering little comfort,
    To savage hearts.

Cherish the moment,
Of love giving and receiving,
    There is no greater gift.

Silence accompanies
Deepest thoughts,
    And enables true sound.

The gong reverberates
Into the ether,
    Attracting hearts to hum along.

It is all predictable,
Sadly, spontaneity
    Is an infrequent rarity.

It requires freedom
And love,
 To open certain doors.

The creative force
That blows out windows,
 Reveals a new kind of seeing.

A moment of perception
Cannot be divided,
 It is neither large nor small.

To an ant,
A grain of sand is substantial,
All beings are subjective.

We are alone
In our quandaries,
Closer together in our joys.

Mount Parnassus poets confer;
Mutually concurring:
Love over words.

It was no more than a shiver
Of hummingbird wing,
    But I knew it was you.

    Waiting to trip me
As I raced
    In my sleep.

    Don't cry beloved,
The false eventually falls away,
    What is true – remains.

We are strongest
When we are present together,
   Love and Presence united.

Winter dark is bitter, loveless,
Summer dark is pregnant with
   Mischievous promise.

The medium of our lives
Ebbing, flowing through time,
   Offers the illusion of reality.

If we were all one race,
One sex, one age;
    A distinguishing factor remains.

Seeing our hypocrisy
Can make us laugh at irony;
    Hilarity causes forgetting.

Divisions exist between
Our hearts and minds,
    Composed of artificial buffers.

Unite inner world,
Outer world
Cannot.

Who are we hiding from
In the grand masquerade?
If not our true selves.

Very little really happens
Of true
Consequence.

The drama of the day
Is much ado about
　　Nothing.

Let your feet follow love,
Joyous and effortless,
　　Like hands on the piano.

Let your voice follow love,
Straight from your heart,
　　To the wild glorious stars.

Wrap yourself in luck;
Cross your fingers, toes, legs,
      To get Presence for Xmas.

Love, though essential,
Must accompany presence,
      And loads of luck.

Shivering may help
Blood circulation,
      Does little for heat production.

Faster than light,
"As soon as think the place"
We are.

Dandelions, ice cream cones,
Summer signals
Return of the full light.

Seeing that you don't exist
Is a first step,
Into unknown territory.

Saying 'I' is a lie,
Likes, dislikes are of the body.
We aren't always watching.

Jumping scales
Can be confusing,
Different truth levels contradict.

Each person's world view
Has something to offer
If spoken from the heart.

The soul is a sensitive film.
Imprinting needs heart,
    Education develops slowly.

To reach higher centers
The soul must be refined
    To a high degree.

Higher centers need
No specific learning,
    They dance to their own tune.

Meher Baba understood war
As a necessary breakdown
Of internal sleep of masses.

On a lesser scale,
Many destructive efforts
Necessary to break up sleep.

Gazing at ruins of inner world,
Not time to rebuild,
But to go deeper inside.

Less me
Is more
You.

Soul blossoms
Flourish in the medium
Of love and compassion.

At a high level
There is no you and me
There is only God.

Makes sense, higher we get
Boundaries between us
Begin to blur.

To actually convey meaning
Is as much work for the reader,
As it is for the writer.

The musical humming
Coming from the bud,
Releases a symphony in bloom.

Simple and silent
Is best,
When all is summed up.

Telling lies on purpose
Not nearly as harmful
As the lie of myself.

Food at each level necessary,
Invisibly fine energy
Needed at cusp of paradise.

It is almost true:
Eat or be eaten.
    Truer is: Eat and be eaten.

Giving to a child,
Is no sacrifice,
    Service from love is joy.

We are critical of others
Rather than facing flaws.
    Sticking points will be revealed.

Difficult issues causing pain,
Possibly better dealt with
By shifting scale.

Transformation, acceptance,
Powerful tools,
To reduce what is not us.

Suffering and ecstasy,
All in between is imprinted on
An evolving learning soul.

Being a scholar is not an end:
Frank observation, searching
For understanding, a beginning.

When we can release
The need to search and strive,
Being becomes joy.

A city of love and light
Fosters the evolution
Of its citizens.

Start a fire
In the depths of your madness,
    It may engulf your emptiness.

Love only hurts
What you are
    Not.

Many virtues,
Graced with health:
    Gratitude joins presence.

Superluminous nimbus
Surrounds with beatitude
The humble, grateful present.

When our light
Joins together and ignites,
It explodes across the globe.

Treat each person as though
You will not see them again,
Because You will not.

Emerging from gestation,
New life spreads its wings,
And soars heavenward.

If it is our last chance,
Take it: Be present.
It is always our last chance.

Each moment offers its own
Direction to take.
There are limited moments.

Open your eyes,
Here is the only place and time
To finally exist.

Snow melts
In the warmth
Of your smile.

Benign spirits gather
Around the crown
Of the god-realized lover.

The final barrier
Is nothing real,
    Only yourself.

The world of duality
Disappears,
    In higher spheres.

Good / Bad
Happy / Sad
    Unite in full realization: God.

Prince and princess
Lead into light
The trimmed-down prepared.

Through the eye of a needle
Squeeze, shrink,
And rejoice in nothingness.

A tiny speck of green
Poking through black earth,
Begins miraculous growth.

Claiming earth, sun, and water,
Plants manifest greenly
In Earth's biosphere.

All things appear
From nothing,
And disappear into nothing.

In our infancy
We are grateful
For life and love.

We live,
We love,
Death enfolds our bodies.